The
Church

ITS CHARACTERISTICS

The Key Truth *The church of Christ is the whole company of redeemed people. Christ is present and active in the church, and uses it for his work in the world.*

It is the church of Jesus Christ (historical)

Through the centuries it is only the church that has experienced the presence of Jesus Christ within its membership. This is because it is *Christ's* church, purchased for himself by his own blood, and cared for as a husband cares for his wife. Jesus declared that where two or three individuals meet in his name there his promised presence would be experienced. No matter how small the group – there is the church.

It is the company of all believers (universal)

This is the church of *different eras;* past, present and future – together, they form the church. It is the church of *different cultures,* found in countries scattered over the earth, but united by its common Lord. It is a church of *different characteristics,* abilities and temperaments; and it is a church featuring *different levels of experience,* from elderly Christians to the newest disciples – yet one church.

It is a unity of the Spirit (spiritual)

The unity of the Spirit, of which the apostle Paul wrote, is more important than the differences of groups and denominations. The church can only truly be one, because of the one Spirit who unites it.

Although all Christians are to work for unity and mend divisions, it is not uniformity nor unanimity that they are to seek. Rather, it is a recognition of all who exhibit the family likeness.

Its authority is God's word (scriptural)

Down the ages the church has had a vital relationship

BIBLE CHECK

Historical Matthew 16:18 Matthew 18:20
Universal Colossians 3:11 Revelation 7:9,10

with the scriptures; it is the scriptural revelation that is the basis of the church's belief and stability.

The church has been commissioned to defend this revelation, to proclaim it, and to submit to its authority. The Bible is the church's authority and tells us all that we need to know about salvation and Christian conduct. On these, the Bible has the final say. On other matters, however, such as church government, there is no clear blueprint – and this no doubt helps to explain the differences existing between churches even in New Testament times.

Its programme is world-wide (international)

The programme of the church is the programme of Christ. Jesus said that his task was to bring good news to the poor and liberation to the oppressed.

When Christ's earthly ministry had finished, he commanded the church to carry out his mission to the world. The Book of Acts shows us the way in which the church's mission expanded from Jerusalem to Judea and Samaria, and then to the whole earth. Our task is one of evangelism and service and to do this, we are empowered by the Holy Spirit.

Its destiny is heaven (eternal)

The church on earth is living between two comings. It looks back to the birth and ministry of Jesus Christ, and it looks forward to his glorious return.

Meanwhile it works in the knowledge that Christ is preparing a future home. On a certain day, known only to God, the trumpet will sound, and the church will be united to Christ.

Postscript *The biblical picture of the church, as described above, helps the church to keep the right priorities in its mission and worship. It also serves as an accurate test to show whether movements and sects which claim to be part of the church are true or false.*

Spiritual Ephesians 4:4-6 John 17:20-23
Scriptural Jude 3 2 Timothy 1:13,14
International Luke 4:16-21 John 20:21 Acts 1:8
Eternal Matthew 24:30,31 John 14:1-3

THOUGHT STARTERS

1 Read Ephesians 4:1-16. What gives the church its essential unity (verses 4-6)? How is this preserved? How does this compare with the kind of unity that Christians should seek (verses 11-16). How is this achieved?

2 A church leader once said 'The church is the only institution in the world which exists primarily for the benefit of non-members.' How far do you agree with this statement?

3 Some Christians strongly emphasise their own church tradition. Others treat denominations as unhealthy. Yet others are indifferent. What is your view?

4 Read 1 Timothy 3:15. What can your own circle of Christian friends do to further the truth of God more?

'We are members of his body' (Ephesians 5:30).

ITS MAIN DESCRIPTION

The Key Truth *There are a number of different pictures of the church in the New Testament. Looked at together, these pictures give us a full idea of the nature and character of the church and its mission.*

A firm building

The New Testament letters take up Christ's theme of 'building' his church – although this idea is not to be confused in any way with literal buildings for Christian worship.

The apostles Paul and Peter, in particular, saw the church as a *spiritual building,* composed of 'living stones' – Christians. This picture shows us how Christians depend upon each other and upon Christ as the building's cornerstone.

A virgin bride

A relationship of deep intimacy is suggested by the New Testament idea of the church 'married' to Christ. We are told that Christ loves the church, and has made it pure and faultless by his death.

The apostle John's vision of the new heaven and the new earth describes the church as Christ's bride, prepared and ready to meet her husband.

A functioning body

The picture of the church as a body, with Christ as its head, emphasises that the church is a living organism and not an organisation.

As in the picture of the church as a building, the *dependence* of the church upon Christ is stressed, but we also learn the important truth that no member of the body is disposable – or of overriding importance.

BIBLE CHECK

Building 1 Peter 2:4,5 Ephesians 2:20-22
Bride Ephesians 5:25-27 Revelation 21:2

A permanent city

The theme of the city of God is usually seen in the Bible as a future hope. God's people live as strangers in the world, and are looking for the city which is to come.

The city of God is mentioned a number of times in the Book of Revelation, where the writer is speaking of the church. When God's chosen people are finally brought to completion, the city will be a vast community of purpose, life, activity and permanent security.

A stable family

The terms 'family' or 'household' of God point again to the relationship that exists in the church between the members and the head. And God's very fatherhood provides a pattern for family life now.

Great encouragement – particularly to Gentile converts in the early church – was found in the fact that all shared equally in the privileges of God's household, Jews and Gentiles alike. No longer was the Gentile an outsider or foreigner. This should also be true of the church today – because barriers spoil the family life God wants the church to have.

An active army

The references to the church as an army are not heavily pronounced in scripture. However, the New Testament teaches that the church is involved in a spiritual warfare.

Intensity, activity and victory are the main ideas conveyed to us by this imagery; the weapons and the victory itself being God's.

Postscript   *It must be emphasised that the church is an organism rather than an organisation, a living fellowship rather than mere buildings, a close family rather than a collection of individuals.*

Body 1 Corinthians 12:12-31 Ephesians 1:22,23; 4:15,16
City Hebrews 13:14 Revelation 21:10-27
Family Ephesians 2:19; 3:14,15 1 Timothy 3:14,15
Army Ephesians 6:12 Revelation 12:11

THOUGHT STARTERS

1 Read and think about 1 Peter 2:1-10. A number of figurative expressions are used of Christians in this passage. Try to list them, and consider their implications.

2 Which of the various descriptions of the church have you found most helpful? Why?

3 Reflect on how much Christ has done for his church, as you consider each picture of the church in turn.

4 Look at 1 Corinthians 12:12-31. What do these verses tell us about jealousy and pride in the church? How do you regard those in your fellowship who seem more gifted, and those who seem less gifted than yourself?

The rocky coastline of Dorset. 'On this rock I will build my church, and the gates of Hades will not overcome it' (Matthew 16:18).

ITS RELATIONSHIP TO CHRIST

The Key Truth   *The life, witness and continuance of the church is totally dependent upon its relationship to Jesus Christ, its builder and protector.*

Christ died for the church

Christ's death is related not simply to individuals, but to the people of God, the church. The announcement to Mary about the impending birth of Jesus was that he would save *his people* from their sins.

It was clear, when Jesus took the cup and gave it to his disciples at the last supper, that he saw his death as bringing a new 'Israel' or people of God into being. Ever since that time, the church has remembered in the Lord's supper the cost Christ paid to found the church.

Christ builds the church

Jesus came to found, not a philosophy, but a community. It was basic to the early Christians' thought that new converts were immediately added to the fellowship; that all who had fellowship with the Father and the Son would be related to one another.

It was more than addition, however. Christ is the very source of the church's life, and so to be in the church is to experience Christ's life in a unique way. By his Spirit he directs the church, gives spiritual gifts to its members and creates unity and love.

Christ protects the church

In the Old Testament God's people were often protected by God, for example, in the story of the blazing furnace in the book of Daniel.

In the New Testament, we are told that Christ protects his people, the church. He defends the church from the attacks of Satan, and preserves it in

BIBLE CHECK

Died   Matthew 1:21; 26:26-29   Acts 20:28
Builds   Ephesians 4:11-16   Acts 2:46,47

adversity. More than this, he provides the power for the church to launch its own attacks against Satan. The church is not on the *defensive* – it is on the *offensive*.

Christ purifies the church

In the Old Testament, some of the prophets pictured Israel as a wife who had been unfaithful to her husband. God's people had been unfaithful to the promises they had made in their covenant with him.

The church is only seen as faithful and pure in the New Testament because of Christ. He has cleansed the church by his death, and continues to keep her holy. We are told that finally Christ will receive the church as a perfect bride, faithful and pure.

Christ intercedes for the church

The word 'intercede' means to act on someone else's behalf as a peacemaker. It is encouraging to know that because of Christ's death on our behalf, he is now in heaven as a man, representing us before the Father.

Because Christ intercedes for us, we are assured of at least three guarantees. First, we are forgiven because of his death. Second, we have free access to God because of his presence in heaven. Third, we are protected against condemnation for our sins by his words spoken in our defence.

Christ prepares for the church

Jesus reassured his friends when he warned them of his departure that they need not be anxious about the future, as he would be preparing a home for them. This shows us that Christ loves the church, and longs to enjoy the company of these who believe in him. His work will not be complete until the church is in the place he has prepared for it.

Postscript *Christ's love for his church led him to give up his own life for her. The church is called to do the same — to submit to the interests of her Lord and to fulfil his will.*

Protects Daniel 3:19-27 Matthew 16:18,19
Purifies Jeremiah 3:6,14 Ephesians 5:25-27
Intercedes Hebrews 7:25-27 1 John 2:1 Romans 8:34
Prepares John 14:1-4 1 Thessalonians 4:16,17

THOUGHT STARTERS

1 Consider the message of Revelation 3:1-6. John is conveying Christ's message to the church in Sardis (in present-day Turkey). How is this passage relevant to the church in general, and to your fellowship today? List the accusations, the challenges, and the promises of these verses.

2 'The Bible knows nothing of solitary religion' (John Wesley). Why should a Christian bother about the church of Jesus Christ?

3 Look at Revelation 1:5,6. What has Jesus Christ done for his church?

4 Read Daniel 3:13-28. What message is there in this story for today's church?

Tromso Cathedral, Norway. 'Christ loved the church and gave himself up for her' (Ephesians 5:25).

ITS AUTHORITY AND MISSION

The Key Truth *The church is not a passive society in the world. It receives its power and direction from Jesus Christ, who has given it his authority to fulfil his mission.*

Guarding the truth

The church is not to create truth, but guard it. It is described as the pillar of the truth; as contender for the faith that has been entrusted to God's people.

Thus the church must follow the apostles both in its standard of teaching and quality of mission. It must do more than guard the truth – it must proclaim it. Equally, it must do more than speak – it must speak the truth. The church is to be scripturally-minded and missionary-hearted.

Correcting the unruly

The Bible teaches that the authority of church leaders must be held in high regard if there is to be healthy discipline in the fellowship. On the other hand, leaders are to be held accountable for their standard of teaching and personal morality.

Indiscipline, immorality and division in the church are not to be condoned. However, all disciplinary measures are to be tempered by the desire to build up the offender and by the forgiveness that surrounds the family of Christ.

Challenging evil

Morally, spiritually and doctrinally, the church of God has always been surrounded by evil. The Bible teaches that evil can be overcome by the power of good. The church must challenge evil by its vigilance and by its determination to live and preach the truth.

BIBLE CHECK

Guarding 1 Timothy 3:15 Jude 3 1 Timothy 6:20
Correcting Hebrews 13:17 1 Corinthians 5:9-13

Evangelising the world

Before he ascended, Jesus gave his disciples a specific command that is to be obeyed by the church in every age. They were to make disciples everywhere, spreading the good news of Christ throughout the world.

We are to announce that Jesus Christ, once crucified for the sins of the world, is alive, and that he is Lord; that forgiveness and the gift of his Spirit are for all who belong to him through repentance and faith. The message is to be proclaimed universally, obediently, relevantly, joyfully and yet urgently. We do it at his command.

Serving the world

Jesus never expected the church to be a proclaimer of words without being a performer of deeds. Christian service is a partner of evangelism, both activities being a necessary part of the mission of God.

Christ is the example for the service that his church is commanded to bring to the world. He fed the hungry, he healed the sick and he brought hope to the despairing. He identified with humanity in all its needs. The same should be true of the fellowship he came to create.

Glorifying God

The church lives for the glory of God. In all that it does, it should direct attention and praise to God. It fulfils this purpose as it bears fruit in faithful service, and mirrors his love.

More particularly, it glorifies God as, following in the steps of Christ, it suffers with him. Jesus said that the hour of his death was the hour of greatest glory. So the suffering and the glory of God's kingdom are combined in Jesus.

Postscript *It is repeatedly in the very weakness of the church that its greatest power is seen.*

Challenging Romans 12:17-21   Jude 19-21
Evangelising Matthew 28:18-20   1 Thessalonians 1:5-10
Serving 1 John 3:17,18   Titus 3:8   Philippians 2:5-7
Glorifying John 12:27,28   1 Peter 4:12-14   Revelation 1:9

THOUGHT STARTERS

1 Read Acts 12:1-19. Consider the church's situation. What were its problems? Its mood? Its influence? Its surprises?

2 Where does the balance lie in practice, for you, between spreading the good news and giving practical service? What adjustments do you need to make?

3 How do you react to disagreements in your fellowship? How far do the words of 2 Timothy 2:23-26 apply?

4 To what extent are you able to take a positive initiative where you are, in being the 'salt' that improves society (Matthew 5:13)?

Cutting through rock, North Wales. 'We are God's fellow-workers' (1 Corinthians 3:9).

ITS ORDINANCES

The Key Truth *Baptism and the Lord's supper were both instituted by Jesus Christ as dynamic symbols of the gospel. The water of baptism signifies cleansing and entry into God's church. The bread and wine of the holy communion signify the receiving of Christ's body and blood, given for us in death.*

BAPTISM

Admission to membership

Ever since Christ's command to make disciples and to baptise them in the name of the Trinity, baptism with water has been the outward distinguishing mark of the Christian.

More than a symbol

When an Ethiopian official was baptised by Philip the evangelist, he was full of joy, although his knowledge of Jesus was limited. Baptism is a powerful event. Received rightly, it becomes a means of God's grace to the Christian.

Death to the old life

Baptism is a farewell to the old life – it is a baptism into the death of Christ. It signifies that the one baptised has been crucified with him, and that the life of sin and self belongs to the past.

Rising to the new life

Baptism is the emergence to the new life; it powerfully speaks to Christians of being raised with Christ, of walking in the light, of peace with God.

Identification with Christ

In his own .baptism, Jesus identified with sinful humanity. In our baptism we are privileged to identify with him, unashamed to be known by his name.

BIBLE CHECK

Admission Acts 2:41 **Symbol** Acts 8:38,39 **Death** Romans 6:3,4 · **Rising** Colossians 2:12 **Identification**

THE LORD'S SUPPER

We commemorate

Christ left us no monument or memorial; he never even wrote a book. What he left us was a fellowship 'meal' by which we could draw close to him and remember the sacrifice of his body and his blood, given for us in death. *This is the backward look.*

We communicate

It is not a dead Christ who is worshipped in the holy communion, but a risen Saviour. As his people share in the bread and wine, they give thanks and praise, and use the opportunity to renew their fellowship with the risen Lord. *This is the upward look.*

We appropriate

Jesus told his disciples to 'take' the bread, as he sat with them. Here is no one-man drama. We are not spectators, but deeply involved; if we come to the Lord's supper with a right attitude, we receive God's grace and strength for Christian living. *This is the inward look.*

We participate

The disciples all drank from the cup, as it was passed from one to another. It is, indeed, a sharing occasion. Believers do not come together in this way merely as individuals, but as a family. *This is the outward look.*

We anticipate

Christ told his disciples that the Lord's supper should be observed regularly – until his return. Then our communion with him will be direct, face to face. Thus the service is a pointer ahead. *This is the forward look.*

Postscript *It is important not to under-emphasise the value of these two ordinances, given by Jesus Christ. Through them we come to a deeper awareness of Christ's death and living presence.*

Galatians 3:27 **Commemorate** Luke 22:19,20 **Communicate** John 6:56 **Appropriate** Mark 14:22 **Participate** 1 Corinthians 10:16,17 **Anticipate** 1 Corinthians 11:26

THOUGHT STARTERS

1 Read Luke 22:14-27. Why did Jesus connect this event with the Old Testament Passover (see Exodus 12:25-27), and with the new covenant, prophesied by Jeremiah (Jeremiah 31:31-34)?

2 Read Acts 16:29-33. In these verses, baptism is shown to be an important event in the Christian's life. Why do you think that baptism is important?

3 As you attend the Lord's supper or holy communion, in what frame of mind should you come – towards Christ himself, yourself, and your neighbour?

4 Pick out the encouraging factors about that evening, and also the discouraging elements. What do they tell us about the gospel and ourselves?

Holly with berries. 'This cup is the new covenant in my blood; do this, whenever you drink it, in remembrance of me' (1 Corinthians 11:25).

ITS MINISTRY AND ORDER

The Key Truth *The church is to maintain a presence for God in the world, proclaiming his message and uplifting his name, under the guidance of appointed leaders.*

Preaching and teaching

The acceptance of Christianity's revealed truth has never been an optional extra in the church. We read in the New Testament of the standard or form of teaching required for growth and discipleship.

The issue of false teaching is dealt with on page after page of the New Testament letters. What protected the infant church was its anchorage in the apostolic teaching, received not merely on an intellectual level, but practised in daily life.

Prayer and intercession

Prayer was the power-house of the early church. It was the unseen weapon that established bridgeheads for the gospel in areas dominated by idolatry and moral darkness.

Prayer is the way in which God's power becomes effective, unhindered by considerations of space, time, culture, or even the prison bars erected by men.

Fellowship and caring

It has been pointed out that the early church was revolutionary. This was not because it roused slaves against their masters, but because it was more revolutionary still – it demolished the old distinctions altogether. The true liberation was freedom in Christ.

People divided by social status, religious background and language now became brothers and sisters in God's household. The apostles taught that widows are of importance in God's family; the sick are to be prayed for, and the hungry fed.

BIBLE CHECK

Preaching Romans 6:17 1 Timothy 1:3-7 Acts 2:42
Prayer Acts 4:31 Romans 15:30 1 Timothy 2:1,2

Worship and praise

Worship is the main purpose of the church. Jesus promised that even where only two or three met in his name, there he would be present with them. Praise and thanksgiving are the distinctive marks of a living church.

The worship of the Christian fellowship is not tied to a building or a structured order, although it is possible that 'liturgies' (forms of worship) were developing by the time the New Testament letters were written.

However the New Testament clearly states that it is not only the leaders who worship God, but all God's people. There is a 'priesthood of all believers', offering spiritual sacrifices.

Leadership and government

In the early church even the precise patterns and titles of ministry differed a little from church to church. Ephesus had 'elders', while Philippi had 'bishops' (both presumably describing the same function of pastoral oversight). There were also 'deacons' who served in a helping capacity, while the apostles were in a class of their own.

Those in the pastoral ministry belong to the church – the church does not belong to them. They are God's gift to the church. They are to feed the flock, they are to be blameless in their beliefs and in their conduct, and their ministry is to resemble that of Christ, who came to be a servant of all.

Postscript   *It is important neither to create a hierarchy, through undue elevation of the leadership, nor to endanger truth and order in the church, through devaluation of those with oversight.*

Fellowship Colossians 3:11   1 Timothy 5:1,2   James 1:27
Worship Colossians 3:16   Hebrews 13:15,16   1 Peter 2:5,9
Leadership Philippians 1:1   1 Corinthians 3:5   Titus 1:5-9

THOUGHT STARTERS

1 Study 1 Peter 5:1-11. List the qualities to be found in one who shepherds God's flock. What was the association in Peter's mind that prompted these terms? Check your answer with John 21:15-17.

2 What are the tensions that the church of Christ inevitably experiences (verses 5-9)?

3 Look at 1 Timothy 4:11-16. These are Paul's words to a young church leader, Timothy. What are the responsibilities and rewards of church leadership? In what ways should we pray for our leaders?

4 Why is the church not a 'democracy'? And yet, why is it not a hierarchy?

Bernese Oberland, Switzerland. 'We have different gifts according to the grace given us' (Romans 12:6).